The Winding Lane Anthology

Enquiries and anthology copies from:
margotmiller@live.co.uk

ISBN 978-1-8382908-2-5
produced by Margot Miller
cover design by Loulita Gill
printed by Flying Colours
Ross-on-Wye

THE
WINDING LANE
Pictures and poetry

Jane Amherst
2021

To my son Michael and
my daughter Elizabeth
who have taught me so
much about the joy and
endurance of living.

FOREWORD
by Jane Amherst

I come from a family linked to the Arts. My father was a musician and so music played a large part in our family life - as well as long, healthy walks up and around Cheltenham. I am the middle one of three girls, and I never really felt part of everyday life. I was a dreamer, and loved the countryside and its beauty of the hills.

My poems are inspired by long, solitary walks making steps and rhythm meld into phrases. The beauty of Gloucestershire and Herefordshire are breathtaking and has enlarged my dream world. I think one needs plenty of time alone to do this and I am grateful for having been given it.

My parents were very supportive and all three sisters joined ballet, drama and music classes. The best thing they did for me was to give me a one-to-one teacher, who entered me for all the LAMDA exams which I passed smoothly - learning and enjoying so much along the way.

When I was still quite young, I was put off writing poetry by a comment that my poems did not scan! It sounded like a death sentence and for the next fifteen years, I wangled my way out of homework to do with writing a poem, until I reached the Rose Bruford College of Speech and Drama. I was horrified when we were told to write a sonnet. I just had to do it. To my amazement, the following week, I was asked to read mine out to the other students.

From then on, poetry played an important place in my life, as it was to all of us at the College. We lived, breathed and moved to poetry.

As time passed, I abandoned competitions, though workshops are interesting and often helpful. For me, the joy is in the writing and sharing. Once the poem is written, it will always exist whether as words on paper or as ash.

December 2020

Jane's Poems

Section II: *The Inner World*   32

Section III: *The Looking-Glass World*   52

I THE NATURAL WORLD

The Winding Lane
(Baregains Lane
 near Ledbury, Herefordshire)

The winding lane meanders quietly
past cows in fields and sleepy bull
it wanders up a gentle rise

spreading scenes before the eye of frosted mists,
muslined trees, hedgerows folded into sky
in gentle, pastel harmony.

Quiet pinks suffuse grey clouds,
and glowing yellow surrounds May Hill,
as the moon faints in gathering light.

Sun breaks, cresting The Ridge,
bursting cloud barriers, firing field furrows.
shooting wonder in a birth breath.

Inspiration from Ast Wood

At the North corner of Ast Wood not far from the hunting gate, in Spring, there is an area of wild daffodils. The swathe is big and shaped like the wing of an angel.

There is discipline in the making of things
and a discipline in the waiting for things,
in the setting aside of busyness
to balance life with silences.

Between the build of the wave and the break of the wave
there is a moment of suspension
and that moment holds necessary power
for the soul's chance of ascension.

Come here with me come here and see
this place in the wood where angels sleep,
wings outspread in giant swathes
on green grass, flecked with gold shimmerings

This is where the earth breathes and leaves rustle at holy tread,
where robins sing in harmony and Spring rises from the dead.
Here is where life starts, in dew drops from the sweating brow,
the woodman's blows on bleeding wood, a cross on which to
                                      hang life's woes.

This is woodland where life rests
between the breaking of the wave,
while smoke from nearby charcoal burn
rises in preparation for the Feast.

To the Warbler

Oh lose me on these rain-drenched hills,
drown me in your rills of song,
warm me with soft feathered down,
safe in hedgerow, homely curled.

Comfort me, oh rain-soaked bird,
winter spring has deceptive touch.
East wind cuts cruelly through
pricked blackthorn in deep flowered snow.

Teach me now to sing once more,
your notes piercing frosted leaves,
teach me to spread strong wings again,
to soar and hover around these hills.

Hover at the stillest point
where air and silence quietly meld,
hear whispered messages from spring,
sense touch in leaf, in heart from Life.

Nature's Intuition

It is understood,
alone in Ast Wood,
the sun in perspective, half a pencil length,
warming trees into full colour,
shooting bluebell leaves in late January air;
it is understood by gnat's
teasing games through tangled hair,
by neat hewn trees, ochre on umber,
stems highlighted, green moss glowing;
understood in spring's ring knowing,
in disappearing shadows,
the hidden skylark's song;
it is understood, it is known,
that winter is almost gone.

To the Ash Tree

When was it your leaves flew
swift as swallows on wind's breath?
Was it not yesterday you were clothed in
showered freshness, dazzling the eye?

I opened curtains to find winter gone
and a song thrush sang high in your tree
welcoming Spring, with such energy,
that I danced through green,
green I could hardly believe,
more vivid, more luscious than ever before.

I must be getting old!
How is it my eyes, my soul
hurt with the beauty that was there?
Now the swallows are gone,
geese flown in V formation
calling and honking as evening set.

The air is full of goodbyes,
grey clouds press on us.
The scuttling mouse searches for warmth.
I will turn on lamps in the darkening room
draw chairs to the fire as stillness descends.
Remember Spring, oh Ash, while we sleep!

The Rising of the Soul

Each moment is a new awakening
or a dying back to earth.

Catching a truth is like catching a fish,
it requires our full attention.

Each touch of your Hand,
each prayer, each moment, brings another,

As the rising of the soul, cloud smothered
breathless from heat haze,
discovers You.

There is nothing worth besides
                        this point of meeting,
beyond comprehension,
it is more than sprung-rhythm choruses
of light space moving,

        It is Silence,
        held in Your Hand,
        waiting the beat,
        learning Your Song.

Spring around Ast Wood

Early, before people stir
and woodlands are free from intrusion,
Nature breathes through wild daffodils.

The world's wrongs are not here,
in the opening windflower
or startled pheasant,
nor in the sun's ice-blinding brightness
piercing round tree trunks
still bare from winter.

Brooding rays *misting* quiet hills
burst through grasses, so brilliant
it doesn't fit categories of knowing,
only The Spirit flowing through day's mysteries,
                              whispers - I AM

Taxol

I am the bringer of life and death,
touch seed and your breath
will cease in a million arrows of
poisoned tips.
Yet,
in the wood,
with the cooing pigeon
and warning bird,
my bark is marked (just as your
breast is
for cutting and radiation).
Be not afraid,
I have the gift of regeneration.
My hundred years holds a single dose
of healing medicine,
I am your wholeness pruned
For more life.   *May 2007*

19

River Severn

The Bore at Newnham-on-Severn

You touch my feelings, invading wave,
gently entering my day's soul,
spreading through this dried out being,
finding levels in small places.
But in the burst of youthful Spring
and final flares of Autumn glory,
you surge over sand, stone and scattered debris
carrying all the careless air,
tossing your head in frothed spray chaos,
stirring mud depths in lashed, swirl passion,
then gently you sigh as your waters spread,
settling into slower rhythms
calmly flowing through the moon's eye.

Yew

I lie a dew drop on a winter's day,
sparkling in ice wonder,
shot by sun splendour,
reflecting dark green from eternal yew.

Hereford Bull
by Edward Kelly

Hereford Bull

That Hereford bull –
he's gone now
shed's empty.

Each day passing the gate, I'd glance to see
and he'd look at me
before turning back to his own thoughts.

Five months standing there in the mud
ambling back for a morsel of hay
he humbled me
because he was master of himself
untroubled by anything of what is or will be

gone now
and the shed bellows his emptiness.

The Foal
*Dedicated to Zoe who has
a special way with horses*

Tumbling from her,
he lies steaming stunned from birth,
a curled concertinaed mass.
She turns and slowly licks away his shock,
unfurling the first stirs of life.

He struggles to stand,
legs splayed out in desperate balance,
wonders how to work four legs,
collapses, struggles and collapses again.

The young girl in her bright pink top,
hair flowing, groomed fresh as a mare's mane,
places a hand quietly on his neck,
settling him from nervous flight.

He charged with cheeky naivety,
cavorting strength from his mother's milk,
confidently nestled against her flank,
stands, a rocking horse waiting to move,

then with skip and a lurch
he's up and away,
flying amongst buttercups
            and apple blossom.

The Whiteleaved Oak
Herefordshire

What is this disturbance of my peace?
Who do you think I am?
Let me tell you,
I am a tree,
a tree,
an old one I admit,
gnarled and broken,
ancient.
I am not here to be gawped at
photographed or revered.
I am just a tree,
no Mystery,
that is from where I was,
before I was,
before you were.
I stand here because that is what it is
to exist
amongst land and sky,
to live to die,
to live again in the deep Mystery.
So why do you hang trinkets on me,
talk of drawing strength
taking my energy?
The Power is found not in ground or air,
                           but - somewhere.

If you sit still in the evening air, if you sit still,
you will hear the water trickling from the trough
singing its own song,
you too will find your own song,
know who you are
leaning on the old farm gate,
gazing at the muddied tracks leading home.
You will sense that you are known
between the dim light and the pheasant's croak,
sharing with him in still air
the absolute certainty that God is here.

I am a tree,
You are you,
God is God,
you are loved,
Him is the answer.

A Painting

My painting will be great slashes of colour on dark tones,
so deep that a wood is hidden in colourbursting vibrancy
and secrets which fold into stillness.

Spirits of earth,
you brown, green atoms,
listen to me.
I cry my folly.
Do not judge my effort,
but glory in your being,
rising to sky so powerfully blue
it overwhelms, like the presence of God.

The Clothes Moth

How quick you are, diverse, fluttering,
weaving into creases, scuttling.
You know how to feint and whisk away
evading my wrathful, clumsy swipes.

You eat clothes so quietly,
chew blouses effectively,
tackling blankets, jackets,
scarves, gloves, stocking packets,
drawing moisture from woven cloth
you terrorist, tiny moth,
wings so fragile dry as law,
yet you destroy the property of kings!

A Blade of Grass

Cool, it touched my warm hand,
infant splendour of newness,
smelling of fresh cut summer lawns,
succulent vegetables, birth gladness.

How fine it was, this one blade,
until the warmth of my hand wilted it,
twisting, curling it into a limp poor thing,
Oh sin!

Moonlight on the Lake
by Sue Locke

In the Night   *8 October 2020*

To think The Three Kings, gazed into this sky
saw the same moon
were guided by stars.

We must see the same stars
to navigate.
Grass sparkles in moonlight.

How can I go into a Home
and be shut away
from this?

Who would let me sit
outside under
the night sky

gaze at the stars,
feel freedom from central heating
and reconditioned air piping?

Just let me breathe this clear, free air,
listen to the owls screech, the trees whisper.

Desolation

I pray for healing
for I cannot help myself,
under grey clouds and sighing wind.

Resting on cracked earth
I watch
the slug creep across grass.

Gnats dance in circles over feverfew,
fired wheatfields wait the cut,
passing traffic throws up dust.

Oh, how great the desolation, dying
on the field's-edge weeds.
I don't much care where I am
so long as the hedgerows sing.

Ragged Stone Hill
September

Sunlit rays pour through sweet mist
Highlighting sycamore branches and leaves from above,
Casting steep shadows on the path below.
Gnats play in nippy air, the atmosphere resting,
A quiet rest.

What has happened to time?
Only yesterday bluebells were here in vivid
                                     purples and blue,
Now juicy blackberries beckon for picking,
Crab apples and plums bubble in jelly,
And there is much bustling below.

For it's market tomorrow in Ledbury,
And folk are squirreling their winter hoard,
Wondering already about Christmas
And will it snow, keeping weather eyes on the horizon,
Shaking heads in winter dread.

But up here in stillness, shadows lengthen,
Dry grasses bend in stirring wind,
Ravens croak, wheeling on thermals,
The rock glows in reassurance,
All is well.

II *THE INNER WORLD*

The New Day

A fresh truth, sprung
from that time
which the Dove's touch
breathes, through unconscious sleep.

We do not know, in the life teaming
sleep, rest,
dark, in our dreams,
that Touch of one heart beat,
and another, to this.

Love in Spring

There are whispers amongst beech leaves,
                          bright with Spring,
as two lovers sit amongst crushed flowers,
with bluebells and aroma of wild garlic opening.

Light falls on them, bright green,
with deeper colours shadowing
the vigorous, rich, growth, foliage scene.

Between them, posed in stillness,
are a thousand, lightning messages
spun, strong as spider's thread,

So quietly they lie,
sung love, in full throated, wild bird song,
no petal stirring to alert the passer-by.

Unforgotten Children

*After the disappearance of little Madeleine snatched from
her bed whilst on holiday in Portugal May 2007 and
media memory from sometime back of a young refugee
girl buried in a few, short minutes after death..*

Thank God for prayers, tears, hearts on fire,
Searches for her hour by hour,
Interviews, messages, world alert
For this three-year-old child snatched, inert,
Dreaming in a foreign land
Playing with waves on holiday sand.

But where were tears for another girl
Lying diseased, unable to curl
On a dirty floor, stomach swollen
With malnutrition and twisted colon,
Alone in crowds of crying need,
Families torn by warlords' greed?

Cameras rolled in both their case,
Known white three-year-old: blank black face,
Churches pealed supplicatory prayers,
Parents faced media stares,
Two clicks only for the other round,
One she lay there, then in the ground.

There was only time to check her pulse,
Then bury her quickly without fuss.
Were there tears for that young soul
Placed without ceremony in a hole?
Thank God for the cameraman who filmed her part
And buried her quietly in his heart.

Choice

This is your life
single
of silence and space
mingling
with nature -
breathing
heart beats
of love for life

Plea

Hello!
Please could I see you because
I'm not coping well
I expect you're busy
But hell
The world has gone crazy
And I'm smothered by walls
Fallen in on me.
You see -
You can't fit me in?
Till -
The following week
Since -
The world has gone crazy
And you're fully booked?
Ah well -
Yes, yes of course
I'll cope.
I hope
You have a good holiday
Bye!
Sigh!
Die inside and smile.

I Wanted to Tell You

for Miles

I wanted to tell you heartfelt things
which I have shut away out of respect for you.
I wanted, on this final goodbye,
to be able to say that I love you,
and I wonder at the prisms of love
creating gentle colours and flashing lights,
how some are real and some are not,
which make the people that we are,

But I just sat there opposite you,
confused and dumb as to what to say,
making polite conversation on this and that,
fumbling my way around your feelings,
wondering what they really were.

I would have thanked you for the good times we had,
but she would come in and interrupt,
with well meaning gestures, irrelevant chat,
and the time passed by, and it seemed
the only thing left was for me to go,
and all I said was, goodbye,

For the words were too sacred for others to hear,
private thoughts for you and me,
the situation most unnatural,
a couple divorced making final goodbyes.
There are so many healings which need to be.
Only eternity will prove them.

Fleeing

Distanced by greyness,
armed with independent drive
I survive,
but sights and echoes of another world
surprise my guard.

Wild daffodils,
nestling amongst dry leaves,
paper cracked from winter,
overshadowed by tall oaks,
whose trunks are lit with mellow sun,
capture me.

Petalled trumpets echo song,
stirring a longing
which is uncomfortable,
a sense of Someone I cannot fathom -

better to ignore it,
if only the song would go away.

Motoring Madness

The carriageway
an endless grey tarmac stretching stretching with
dust dots zipping
and a ricochet whiz of overtaking cars
flashing down the fast lane.
As they pass the overhead speed signs
        warn

SLOW   SLOW

ACCIDENT

We creep at walking pace, jostling positions for the second phase race,
frustrated at our wasted time,
passing funereal the emergency line
with the zombie figure, her wrecked car a zapped fly, she standing
suspended by
        time
            in shock
Wondering why the brakes locked to make her skid,
        unable to comprehend the dead kid
            silent
         in her tin coffin.

There is a flicker of recognition in our passing cars, a gasping,
                         an asking
"who are they, were they?" as we head for our holiday destinations
or important financial meetings,
driving carefully for the next five miles
        at least
            until

released by the signs, we surge forward to catch the time we lost
blanking the spectacle on the motorway verge.

ON FEELING ILL

Today the rain is beautiful,
a telephone ring of droplets
falling on clay soil-hardened.
I stir a cracked body,
bones dry, throat sore,
gritted eyes blinking,
but, oh the delight of living
when rain falls.

Now I will grow
from my comatosed brain,
stand alone in falling rain
with fingertips stretched up high,
feeling water fall in streams
down my arms.
And what if tomorrow I die?
Today, I have been dancing in water.

Rest

Do not disturb the old man's quiet rest,
problems startle like the plover from her nest
shooting up in the air, tumbling to earth,
calling the tractor with all her worth,
oncoming, oblivious
               to spare her eggs.

Let the old man rest gently in his chair,
seeming asleep, yet in the air
soaring through memories of the past,
balancing the plough, guiding the horse,
pausing to rescue the eggs in their nest,
lifting them lightly with weathered hand,
before placing them gently in turned stubble,
whistling assurance to the frantic song,
her peewit cry,
               long gone.

The land is different today
as machine stricken fields lie uninhabited.
Targets are met and the earth cradles bones,
plovers have gone
               and with them our souls.

Do not disturb the old man's quiet rest
with scenes of this world's madness,
let him turn at the gate, survey the ploughed field
and watch the plover
               fly back to her nest

January 2008

ON THE POEM

A poem is like soft clay
moulded on the wheel
touch it too much and it collapses

Parting in Autumn

My daughter leaves
for university 2003

The poignant moment of parting comes,
with lingering longings to remain with her,
sends echo waves of contracting pain
in the silent, sanctuary of the womb.
Whirlwind anguish rises
as autumn leaves fall like tears,
watering beauty no longer shared -
quenching the desert drought in sorrow.

Birds still sing
the sun still shines
a gentle breeze lifts a strand of hair
and life beckons to
carry on
though she is gone
to a new adventure.
It's like a death
and not a death

and I wander like a ghost along
The Bromsberrow path we went before -
only alone now,
and the geese fly too
in perfect rhythm
their wings sing
making music in the air.

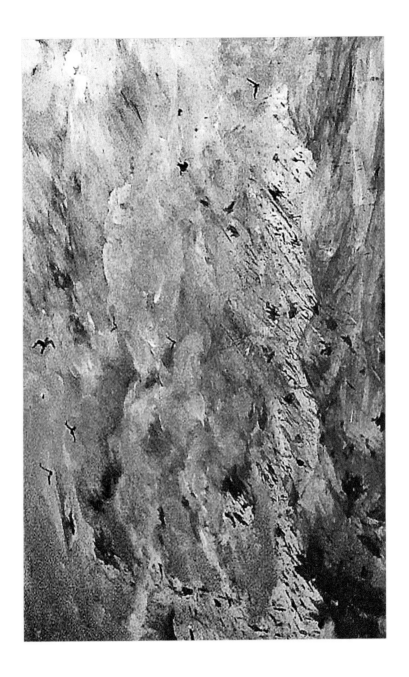

The Ordinary Things

When traumatic things happen,
the world becomes estranged,
ordinary things rescue, for you to hang on to,
simple things, which are solid as oak.

How tedious they seem in good times,
making beds, washing up, emptying bins,
tidying, paying bills, going to work,
taking that same journey day after day, in traffic jams.

How we long for a change from them,
a new perspective, different scene,
a break in the chain, a holiday!
But things are different now.

Like the toddler learning to walk, balancing against
                                 ordinary things,
you steady yourself from the waves of emotion
surging and crashing, threatening to destroy,
hold on to the ordinary things, for they rescue.

Standing in your latter years, solid as oak,
looking back on that extraordinary time,
remember the tears and anguish quietly.
look back, and you will see
that you carved beautiful things,
                from the ordinary.

Pixley Church, Herefordshire

A sketch of a moment
hastily drawn
with a message of something not quite defined
-alerting the soul, body, mind -

in a robin's song,
gravestones,
snowdrops sheltering
in the ivy-covered, tumbling wall,
the open church waiting.

In stillness I stand, quietly breathing,
smell lingering incense, honey bees buzzing,
plainness and shot-colour shine
through the east lancet window,
portraying our Lady with Gabriel speaking.

Last week's hymn numbers are now redundant,
unlit candles in holders stand waiting,
a little vase of flowers on a windowsill droop,
and there is hope in them, the hope of Love.

The Healing

Let Me pull the thorns from your head
so you can pull them from Mine.

In time there is Birth
each hour Good Friday
and all is Easter
in the rising day.

Life fullness is met in tough gentleness
as harebells tremble in hillside winds.
The child sleeps peacefully in its mother's womb,
while spiders weave glistenings on meadow grass
and pain ricochets through cats' jaws
crunching trembling, stricken mice.
The laws of nature never fail,
but we blind people do, and ail,
unable to trust, refusing to accept
that letting go, its an absolute must
to be rescued from the cliff face.

I will be still as You pull out the thorns,
sit quietly with You in my recovery,
turn and see You,
no longer blind,
admire Your Face so kind, so beautiful
and know You in glory.
I will be with You in harmony
singing Your song
as You sing mine.

Depression

Allow me to sink to the bottom of this pond,
I am dying inside from a gangrenous wound.
The waters are murky,
it is hard to see,
I need no diagnosis,
I just need to be.
Darkness encloses as I descend,
life has bludgeoned me,
I wish it to end.
If you pull me up now as I'm halfway down,
you *will* destroy me and I *will* drown.
Do not interrogate or use clever words,
my senses are numb, language blurred.

Gently I sink into shadowed sand,
I am not cursed, I am not mad,
I have merely returned to the dark of the womb,
where water surrounds me and I am home.
Nine months it took before I was born,
give me time to develop before I return.
Now I rise up to light and to air,
I am different now, free from despair.

The Listener

He knew it was genuine,
he knew it was bad
and he saved me,

picked up the receiver,
stopped the persistent ring
which stuns the ears,

and he listened,
said how glad he was to be there, listening

and it calmed my fears,
so that I was quiet
and did things I don't normally do

reading a book by the open fire,
letting the dog pull the socks from my feet,
killing them dead

so that I laughed,
and happiness flowed in place of fear and
that thing disappeared.

III   *THE LOOKING GLASS WORLD*

Church Cat

The village church was in such a mess,
parishioners in despair,
for infestation of mice was such
that they were everywhere.

The pest man looked quite gloomy and
showed them his despair,
"This particular outbreak
is a type extremely rare.

"The poison'll not get rid of 'em,
they've grown immune to that.
The thing which might just do it
is, "Get an old farm cat,"

The PCC said "Good idea",
(for most church records tell,
cats were employed by clergymen and
gave all field mice hell.)

So they found a handsome ginger tom
and sat him in their midst,
he answered to the name of Rum, and
seemed to get the gist.

He sat so neat and upright,
sporting a massive chest,
his tail flicked ever so slightly,
and whiskers twitched in jest.

He was entered in the records with
an allowance for his needs, which
included food and bedding and an
antidote to fleas.

After lots of speeches of welcome,
a hug from old Miss Rudge,
a ringing peal from the tower,
a nod, a wink, a nudge

as if to say, you'll do it mate,
you'll rid the mice for us,
they went home in their motor cars
and forgot about the fuss -

till, that is, come next Sunday,
when they turned up at the door,
the warden promptly fainted
at the chaos on the floor

for the mice had wreaked such havoc
that it became a famous case,
and was televised on all channels
as *The Church Cat in Disgrace*

He hadn't bothered to do a thing,
he really quite liked mice,
and the home he'd just been given
was really very nice.

I mean, why bother to work at all
when you've been granted every whim,
his bed was extremely comfortable
and was sloth such a sin?

The warden wanted to throw him out,
for he hadn't earned his keep,
but dear Miss Rudge, who held no grudge,
began to beg and weep,

For she was such a lonely soul
and had no one at home,
so could she have poor Rummy
and be no more alone?

This suited all who heard her plea
and Rum was pleased as punch,
it fitted his bill nicely
and he knew there would be lunch!

The Restless Sleeper

Ahhh, it's good to get into my bed
the bottle's warmed it well,
the bit my bottom sits on
is like the fire from hell.

But, oh my feet, they feel like ice
wrapped in sheets of snow,
so I'll sacrifice my backside
for the bottle on my toe.

I hope I don't get chilblains,
it's hot and cold does that,
I'll sort of touch and stroke It
like the clawings of the cat.

Oh bother, that reminds me,
I didn't let her in,
she'll wake the neighbours in the night
with her yowling and her din.

I'm just all warm and cosy,
she really is a bore,
but if I use the loo as well
I won't be up at four.

Right into beddy-byes again,
I'm shiv'ring with the cold,
let's make the pillows comfy
and give my neck a mould.

No that's not right, it's lumpy
and pressing on my cheek,
let's give it a good old bashing
then sleep until next week.

Hang on, have I damped the fire
and twiddled the air vent shut?
did I? didn't I? I'll have to check
or I could be roasted nut.

I throw myself back into bed
with the force of a charging horse,
switch off the lamp, snuggle down
then think of something worse.

I haven't locked door at front,
a burglar could just walk in,
he could rifle my belongings
and commit a carnal sin,

I mean, I know I'm not attractive
with my face all smeared in cream,
my hair done up in rollers
it'd be enough to make him scream

Could that be classed as self defence
or going over the brink?
I'd hate to be charged with *causing*
            mental trauma to the intruder
and ending up in clink!

I'm feeling too warm and cosy
to go downstairs to check,
he could be a dishy burglar
so really, what the heck!

My toes are really hot now
and so is the rest of me,
I'm sweating twenty buckets
and need a cup of tea.

I suppose a glass of water
would be a better drink,
tea is such a stimulant,
I might not sleep a wink.

It's 2AM., I'm still awake, the
world is fast asleep,
my bedclothes are in disarray
and I'm lying in a heap.

I've read a book, stroked the cat,
drunk tea with a lot of rum,
listened to the radio,
am feeling really glum.

Soon the light will turn to grey,
and dawn will wake the world,
but I'm asleep a snoring heap
with cat on pillow curled.

Cheque Book Drama

I have such weeks of muddles,
when all I seem to do,
is spin, spin, spin around
then spin around anew.

I am *just so* disorganised
don't put things away,
dump the papers on the floor
to sort some other day.

But now I'm in a quandary,
my cheque book's disappeared,
I put it by the table,
it all seems rather weird.

It was here from last night's meeting
when I signed out cheques galore,
then dumped it with those papers
by the table on the floor.

So let's go through the muddled pile,
it must be somewhere here,
Oh look! The electric bill
from December of last year.

Goodness, did I pay it?
I really must find out,
I can verify the cheque stub,
If the wretched book's about.

Cowpats! I'll retry the floor pile,
turn out the cupboard next door,
the upstairs, downstairs, garage,
and recheck my bag once more.

Three hours of searching and looking,
interspersed with some glasses of wine,
my eyes are googly and blurry
and I no longer walk in a line.

I sink to the floor despondent
with aching head in hands,
I wish I were somewhere special,
an exotic island with sands,

Still this is getting me nowhere,
I'll go through the papers once more,
methodically calmly and slowly ---
Hey presto it's here on the floor!

Sitting between the insurance
the gas bill, minutes and grime,
this calls for a celebration
and another goblet of wine.

I'll put it away in a minute,
just ring my sister first,
she'll be so relieved I've found It
and the problem's not any worse.

Epilogue

It's been so good to chat to her
I'll take her wise advice,
Now where did I put that cheque book?
I can't lose it in one day twice!

Strawberry Fields - Herefordshire

The Strawberry Thief on a Herefordshire Fruit Farm

'DO NOT EAT THE STRAWBERRIES'
The notice firmly decreed,
'For if you do it's stealing
And a serious crime indeed.
Anyone caught doing so,
Will suffer the consequence sure,
For this firm won't mess with criminals
And you'll feel the hand of The Law.'

This was written in seven tongues
For all workers to understand,
For the owner must make a profit,
And carefully manage his land.
The notice was taken seriously,
Not a strawberry consumed on site
By the working pickers in endless rows -
Except, for the squirrel, at night!

Now he couldn't read the paper,
He didn't really care,
The succulent smell was good,
And he'd a hungry family to rear.
He sat in his dark tree hollow
Twitching his sensitive nose,
Listening for human workers
To leave the enticing rows.

When the dusk descended at bedtime,
When all were tucked in bed,
He ran down his gnarled oak tree trunk
And allowed himself to be led
To the yawning mouth of a tunnel,
With its goodies so well displayed,
And he popped along each tender plant,

Picking at this and nibbling a seed,
Breaking a stalk, feeding his greed;
My! they were good these bright, red things,
They were woppers, gob stoppers, a harvest galore,
He chewed and he feasted and gobbled some more,
Then with paws full of strawberries,
And one in his mouth,
He set off back homewards
To his tree facing south.

When the farmer discovered the awful truth,
He blew his top, he hit the roof.
He took out his gun to shoot the thieves,
But all he found were squashed oak leaves,
For Nature cares nothing for profit and stuff,
It's the clever and strong and them that's tough
Who survive with her. No!
She simply lured them to cherry trees,
Where they happily gorged in a morning breeze!

Financial Phobia

On this twelfth day of May
in two thousand and ten,
I have to face high finance
and I'm like a worried hen.

My nest egg's disappearing,
the tax man collects a lot,
and if I'm not too careful,
I'll have an empty pot.

I invested in some companies,
it all seemed jolly fine,
the man explained for ages
before I signed the dotted line.

I really couldn't tell him,
I didn't understand
a single word of gilts and bonds,
that my head sank into sand.

But now I have to face it
and see what's going on,
I've dodged financial language for
way, way, far too long.

My desk is piled with coloured files
from powerful companies,
I've briefly glanced at pages,
and it means nothing at all to me.

An awful crash is coming.
the rich will eat the poor,
and when they find they're hungry
they'll look around for more.

I'm off to live in woodland,
learn language from the deer,
the fox, the badger, wary hare,
no blogs or pods are there.

But echoing through the glory
of a bluebell wood in May,
are mocking notes from a cuckoo,
who has to have his say:

'Cuckoo,' he calls, 'stupid lot,
about to lose your face!
I've tipped out your investments and
I've a woppa in their place.

'Oh I can cheat and camouflage
better than any of you, don't look so
astonished, cuckoo, cuckoo, cuckoo!'

As I sit and ponder this
gazing all around,
I wonder what the answer is,
where wisdom can be found.

It's certainly not in Nature
or much of the human race,
wisdom is a spiritual gift
and can only come from Grace.

As for my predicament,
I'll pray, then have some lunch,
ring up my advisor
and discuss the credit crunch!

The Hypochondriac

Mornin', Doctor, yes it's me again,
me stomach ain't arf giving me pain.
I've taken them sachets as you suggest
but the pain's moved up from my knees to my chest!
an the wind, excuse me, is somethin' awful,
even the dog looks at me all baleful.

I said to Mike, it's not the grub,
but he just grunts an goes down the pub,
that's the last I sees ov'im till six
just as I'm havin' my evening fix.
Them big, red woppas don't arf give me grief,
placiba somethin' you say for relief?
My arse more like it! Excuse me,
it's the stress and the jip I'm gettin' yer see.

You'll give me some blue ones to try instead,
take two before I go to bed?
Well, I hopes they work, I don't sleep so well,
pain in me toe is givin' me hell,
yes, it started last Tuesday on me mornin' shift
Pushin' them trolleys up to the lift,

Now, that brings me to the spot on me nose,
I've not got acne I suppose?
This global wotsits quite a worry,
but I'm doin' my bit by not eating curry
and cuttin' down fags to twelve a day,
so that should help me tooth decay.

Five minutes up, I've got ter go?
but you ain't yet looked at my swollen toe!
You can't just finish this consultation,
I haven't yet mentioned me constipation,
varicose vein, me waxed up ear,
an don't go tellin' me it's all just fear
anxiety thingy and in me head,
I'm sure by Christmas I'll be dead.

Next Tuesday, then. I'll bring my list,
an we'll go through all the bits you've missed.
It'll be a locom as you're on a course?
The NHS is gettin' worse
Well, I'll see yer again wiv a bit o luck,
Cheerio, Doctor, pecker up!

The Dragon's Protest

A protest against a
communications company
erecting a mast on the Malvern Hills
for the use of mobile phones

"There're dragons on the hill, " I said
They thought I was clean out of my head,
The Planners stopped. The Planners stared.
The dragons were hidden.
Who cared?

"Do dragons exist?" a Councillor asked,
I reacted pretty fast,
"Through millions of years they have survived.
They live secretly on this ancient hill,
With mystery and history surrounding them still.
Please leave them alone to guard the past,
Let stillness remain, let silence last."

But the Councillor laughed and shook his head,
"Dragons are dead these days," he said.

Then one day men came to clear woodland away,
Cut down old oaks, and had their say,
"A perfect position to erect a mast.
Bollocks to daydreams, to fairy tales past!"

The transmitter beamed its waves of sound
The wild life shuddered - hid in the ground,
Outrageous progeny were born to men
The dragons flew off to another den
Wonderful phones, modern technology
Creating new problems, ending in tragedy.

There's a new dragon on top of the hill
It's not a friendly one
This one can kill!

The woods below St.Baume cave/church, Provence, France 2011

ILLUSTRATIONS

ACKNOWLEDGEMENTS

Thank you to Sue Locke for springing into action when I said I wanted to make a book, immediately recommending Margot Miller. This was the best idea Sue could have put forward. We have worked easily together, with a natural understanding of what is needed and a mutual enthusiasm for the project.

I would like to thank my friends Margaret Morse from Whiteleaved Oak and Carole Thornton from Chaceley for their encouragement over the years, and my husband Jonathan for seeing me through.

Many thanks to the artists who allowed me to include their pictures: Jenny Jones (*ash, yew* and *oak*), Edward Kelly *(bull)*, Sue Locke (Orlando and *Moonlight on the Lake*), and Margot Miller (*pheasan*t and dragon).

Jane Amherst - December 2020